MW00437396

Daily Sonnets

Also by Laynie Browne

POETRY

Original Presence (Shivistan Books, 2006)

The Desires of Letters (Belladonna, 2006)

Drawing of a Swan Before Memory (University of Georgia Press, 2005)

Mermaid's Purse (Spuyten Duyvil, 2005)

The Desires of Letters (g - o - n - g Editions, 2005)

Webs of Agriope (Phylum Press, 2004)

Nascent Toolbox (with Lee Ann Brown, The Owl Press, 2004)

Pollen Memory (Tender Buttons, 2003)

Gravity's Mirror (Primitive Editions, 2000)

Clepsydra (Instress, 1999)

The Agency of Wind (AVEC Books, 1999)

L O R E (Instress, 1998)

Rebecca Letters (Kelsey Street Press, 1997)

One Constellation (Leave Books, 1994)

Hereditary Zones (Boog Literature, 1993)

FICTION

Acts of Levitation (Spuyten Duyvil, 2002)

Daily Sonnets

Laynie Browne

Counterpath Press
Denver, Colorado
2007

Acknowledgments.

Grateful acknowledgment is made to the editors of the following publications, where some of these poems originally appeared: *B after C, Cranky, Dusie, mag, Five Fingers Review, Golden Handcuffs Review, Mem, Parthenon West Review, Titanic Operas, Traverse,* and *Wandering Hermit Review.* The poems "How About Some Chair for Breakfast" and "Why I'm Not A Paintbrush (or L.A. Sonnet)" appeared as a pamphlet from No Press. Poems from the "Ascidian Heart" series originally appeared in the online journal *The News.* Poems from the "Sonnets of Aristotle" series originally appeared in *Inscape.* Poems also appeared in the anthologies: *Bay Poetics,* edited by Stephanie Young (Faux Press), and *War & Peace 2,* edited by Judith Goldman and Leslie Scalapino (O Books). Many thanks to Lisa Jarnot, Judith Goldman, and Denise Newman for readings of this manuscript, and to Julie Carr and Tim Roberts of Counterpath. Thanks to all of my collaborators and conspiratorial aides, especially Brad, Benjamin, and Jacob Davidson.

Counterpath Press
Denver, Colorado
www.counterpathpress.org

© 2007 by Laynie Browne. All rights reserved.

Printed in Canada

Library of Congress Cataloging-in-Publication Data

Browne, Laynie, 1966–
    Daily sonnets / Laynie Browne.
        p.   cm.
    Includes bibliographical references.
        ISBN 978-1-933996-00-4 (pbk. : alk. paper)
I. Title.

PS3552.R748D35 2007
811'.54—dc22

                                                      2006037256

Contents

To Benjamin and Jacob, my daily sonneteers
inventors of the "real time sonnet" and "dailiness"

Daily Sonnets

1

Pirates attack ships in Malacca Strait
Missing her front or frontage beam
You rearrange the particles in your wake
Missing solvent overtures
She carves her way in with a face
Not luminous but pressing, present
You've borrowed my height, my nouns
And now my nomenclature
Crown mistaken for crumb
Under diminutive table sent
Pluck disobedience like a cowl
Be monster, bug, horse
I am slowness compelled to utter
With half the world's oil

Covered in vinegar lists
It's very Bob or Elmo
Off with your sling
Are apostrophes incorrect birds?
Unsent attachments
and I have this toddler
We've traveled removing
our metal parts
I'm mad at your shirt
Useless clod
J. learns to gallop
Practicing in airports
If you catch up
Please remind me of everything

I have a friend I'd like to see who exhausts me
When we went away it was still summer
I was still myself wearing this circlet to bed
Not only a distant relation to a person I once knew
Now J. is galloping to toss his blue cup
B. is thinking we might both have gone out
Leaving no one
Hearing everything as a kind of dinnertime entertainment
He played harmonica, slide recorder, and zucchini
While J. danced and did interpretive downward dog
Then we washed
And showed them their beds
This music repeats itself night after noon
Accompanying affectionate newts in all endeavor

F Dictionary Sonnet

Floodgate, light drowsy particles
Containing a stream or a torrent
Of various other flatfishes or a small fleet
Wider than a ruffle, a barefoot sea
Low pressure almost unnoticeable
Form or manner
Small loyalist letters
Diamond shaped at the point
Of maximum ebb
Perspicaciously marked with initials
Of an ancient empire, its people or language
Paleozoic, occurring from light bantering talk
Characterized by the existence of many reptilian
Successors, elusively thin or tenuous

C *Dictionary Sonnet*

Tailcoat take a sharp pointed
Microscope, midsummer in arctic
Of mid-calf length
A quiet plodding horse
Ditto a forked stick useful
In locating underground
Birch or semiprecious biographer
Come semi-monthly titular vizard
Resembling glass, as in glossiness
Unknown or exhaustive vulture
Condole a rounded protuberance
On bone
Confabulate a person who makes or sells candies
Confessedly to keep within bounds

You never sit on the carpet in this game
You can sit wherever you want to sit
Depending on where I make the stream of cards
You sit where the stream is not
What we arrest the story sees comingly
When we depart we answer another department
When we weep we are also
eating some proclivity
I cannot disappear from circumstances
where I'd like to find myself least
Why is it difficult to throw away a cracked wine glass
Not because I love its company
A broken tone of voice, a break without
complete separation of parts

Half Sonnet + 1

The little water that conquered the world
I don't have stories when I have my clothes on
My household is too malleable
This whistle isn't for whistling
Tables come and go, ants, guests
Calls about fraud, no space in swim class
Observing negativity in kindergarten
A long drink from my toothbrush

My belt pushed the tinder closer
Almost in the middle of the table
Silver lead ores from nearby
A cord with a corner torn
I made a pile near the cavemouth
You want to draw him
There is but one thing we know
She was unable to assume
The manner
That would have made her absurd
Avoiding the long tusks
Gone never to return
Wrenched from my hands
The other sledges with crunch-runners

Constancy is my daylight
supposition where you suppose
these hands may carve
tunnels in dough
In question, small hands
more than my own
searching weightlessly
constantly asking askance
offering what may not be
willed, but given
A cup steadying something
which the hand cannot
Little hand you are my constancy
As you require I do not waver

Events don't change time
One strap on one visitor off
If I think in other words I turn to dust
I want the morning to erase this night
I wish in homily
Tired is forgetting a song
Uncertainty is rapid
Being divinity isn't easy
Even though you may think
I'm learning my job description
Now you learn your job description
In the meantime I'm supervising myself
Please forgive me,
imaginary salary

Love Sonnet to Light (half-imagined)

You look about five
Except for the beard
Lying in bed worrying
Over a short in your
Fairy light
Too young to read
While you brood

Go to ablutions
Say sorry before you run over Elmo
Apply uniformly before the very idea
Yields the finest rice for injured birds
Conventional farmers burn entire fields
Of walking distances
Ask your doctor about blithe pond books
Our war on making the letter relevant
Once again I expect enclosed critics
Punk unseen matter correction
Working through carnal decoration
Pay attention mystery guest
Rimbaud is drowning in this
Estuary century

Benjamin Makes a Shoebox-Mummy in Preschool

Flashlights are as good as
Grief, magnesium phosphorus
A toddler locks himself in an office
Can fix me eventually
He was running to make his mummy
And fell
I cannot describe her taking leave
From her body, and yet
Proximity is a first-hand remedy
Suppose he wakes up with this picture in mind
Sister is trolley to embalming
He rubs the body with resin and salt
Preserve nothing which sitting won't exhaust
Suspend regular action and replace speech with _____

Sonnet of Aristotle

"The following creatures have large hearts: the hare, the deer, the mouse, the hyena, the ass, the leopard, the marten, and practically all other animals whose cowardice is either outright or else betrayed by their mischievous behavior."

—Aristotle

LATENT SONNET-IMPRINT

When an object approaches the eyes
the eyelids close
The slipper limpet strains such
particles from the present

The infant runs to its
cloth-mother when
forced to display bowers
of the satin bower-birds

Your response to a slight pinprick
or sickle dance at the entrance
to the oyster beds
where we can be serious

Starlings in flight tighten their formation
marking the first *true sense organs*

15

Sonnet of Aristotle

A DIAGRAM ILLUSTRATING THE COMPARISON BETWEEN
THE SKELETONS OF HUMAN AND BIRD

The earth's rotation once ruined
astronomy

After all manner of mathematical
subtleties—wrapped in

silk while still alive
stronger than steel threads

of the same diameter
An error of eight or nine

minutes—
and the ninth sphere

would no longer be
necessary

Its coloration matches the petals
among which it lies

16

I'm looking for Mongolia
Write down this song
Are you writing down this song?
Robots are fixing a horse
Doesn't it sound like somebody hammering?
Robots are taking a walk in the forest
A flamingo walking on hind legs
A lion on the plains
More than one place touched
Angola in your mind is yellow
You are dancing in a big square
With an empty middle
Touch the purple arrow
A different Mexico

Sonnet Beginning with a Line from
Anselm Berrigan

My model personality slams into the side of quaint
   signature daisies
Mocking a bunch of birds who left and forgot to take
   their feathers
A dog referred to by one's child's name
Alphabet up a tree
My mock runways flew down
To admire confident women after surgery
When I'm nursing I don't worry about terrorism in
   Jerusalem
Or a neurological condition that interferes with attic rats
My muck psychobiology
Slams into the side of summer's veil
Bound to function—give me that thimble Miss
There will be tracks
And taking the needle out of the kerchief
She set to work again on the floor

7 *Sources Sonnet*

Coward, I spoke in Cherokee; If I were on my feet
As a way to punctuate the world
She's reveling in her single status
Everything comes when it must come
At 5 o'clock in the morning it was still quite dark
Kaffir lime, acacia
You are the shoreline
Huddled below a low earthen bank
As if to wear the world
Despite a snogging session
In one a bridge collapsed
Heterogeneous plainly dressed persons were sitting at it
Fast forward rather than flashback
These granules which are inside the absorbent padding

Post-Election D Sonnet

A dumb duration that enters
The body, used to color textiles
Paper, hair, dyed-in-the-wool
Dutch uncle subject to dust storms
A cloth brush for removing duplicate
Dumps, dumplings or dumbfounded
Pennyweights used to designate
Difficult shortwave reception
To cause to appear smaller in size
Character, a couple or pair of
Dungeons pertaining to twelfths
A person easily duped, dipped
Into coffee, denim fabric, to make a
Speechless collection of ammunition

Homeopathic Yellow Pages

Remember, you're a bad guy
I want my head on
My hood
Even in death, "daring man"
Craves his ladder
The skull is a blueprint of lifestyle
From the front fin of the earliest fish
Afraid of its own bones
Mail arrives from Egypt
Silver dolphin treasures
She's slipped out of her coma
Paralyzed
We mummify a lamb
Build a pyramid

21

Love Sonnet To Light

Here are the questions I did not ask
And why I did not ask them
Do you read my thoughts
Continually as a practice
Or more spasmodically
As the line begins to waver
Do you speak to clarify
My aspiration
If I look down at the page
Will I remain unseen
Yet magically present like the seeker
Who is certain you speak
to him privately
As I speak to you

It's great to be a drawing
Because I can be anything
What's wrong with being a drawing?
The man who drew too much
Why not be with old friends always?
That was great imagining Dorothy
Of your mommy and daddy
We all have bodies
When I rub my eyes I see the colors
I'd like in an evening gown
The breeze looks like lions
This book smells like the loft
In which you cure
Your vowels

Sonnet Written with Lisa Jarnot

This is a rare word
used only in the game of golf
"prattle" the act of shrimp-like
public relations, of involving or
related to the antelope
on sloops out in the wavy sea
mute proclamations of the ant bear
occupy my antidote to
reign in the bird calls
to reign in the moon and sun and
become describable off-street parking
very near #9 bus route and percussionist
watercrafts, hovering, harmonic
swinging on the sea

Superman wants his milk
A baby astronaut
Bob, and other contractors
Lie face down on the carpet all day
Once there was a robot
Hiding in the bushes
And there was a superhero
Hiding in the treetop
There was a bear in a house
Made of tar
Once there was a bear
Living in a bear
Bears don't live in bears
Hiccupped himself into a fire

The human body absorbs sound
Will be followed
Looked after passing your pencil
Shoulder fibrous
With muddy unrecognition
Why do I require these sudden
Tablets of concentration
She made poetry sound like a playdate
Squeezing her wrought hands
I thought she might jump
This little bit of Telegraph Ave. vibe
Faces selling as if brand were personality
Obstinate opera
Literary war council

26

Sonnet of Baron Marc Selys Longchamps

ASCIDIAN HEART

Ancestry of Vertebrates

The heart is that oracle
out of which rope is made vessels
sobrieties of the world since altered

Night mitten invert
all small reigned
well salted ailments

Out of the great variety of phyla
the vertebrate stem arose
ancestor of "mother"—endocardium
Bebra wrote a description from his cabin window

It is dark, but for illumination
of the submarine world

Pyrosoma   at the surface
makes visible   sails, masts, rigging

Sonnet of Baron Marc Selys Longchamps

ASCIDIAN HEART

The heart then is mal de mer
with fretted neck
the quality of shining
a rare metallic earth element

abundant in growth as vegetation
to lie hidden
to go furtively
as with a sword

One trove beatific
a sudden trip or roll
does not separate on standing
with only a single tunic garment

Beasts in the sky meliorate your way
Carousels reply insipidly to tears

Post 9/11 Sonnet (2003)

Before eleven was a number it was an object
Floating through continuum to claim its authority
The number became an event I could not at first recognize
As I nursed my two-week old infant
Without rest the mind lacks a certain elasticity
Unbearable fragility as refuge
He slept easily
Unlike my first
Notion of terrorism
Primarily a lack of previous
Outrage from citizens regarding
Atrocities, as if elsewhere, earlier did not exist
Or any other date so immortalized by terror
From within these self-obsessed states

I have a great sense of expectancy today
Perhaps I am about to be disappointed
Or perhaps the datura of mind drops
Like this fountain before me
Otherwise not insidious world events
Alarm me and my own expectancy
Is in walking among them easily
As if there were time to walk in a garden
Or to sit, now where I belong
A little bird drinks from your fountain
Then another, losing track of the line
Each phrase a continuous middle
The first time I arrived, with no middle
Entranced with no mind of the line

Finished severation asthma countryside course
Toil haymaking and slaughtering
Grotesque creatures, moments
Thought was body
Perhaps exhaust commonplace movement
Seems space thought I
Was too young
Compressed frivolous clerking
Bit reader joined this detest
Revered interview
I am likely to be blamed
You can't but shut agreeing man
You know the end my wishes admit
Conjurer

Light on the coverlet
This non-reliable rain
Are we talking or are you reading
True expression is in your
Leaning back abruptly into pillows
Not what you say as you say anything
Not cognizant of who will
Pick up after the raw provocative
Underthings of thought made chaste
Just what sort of undernetting did you suppose
Not able to concentrate at the hour
Of true concern
We have this habit of not embracing
Shall I read you?

Love Sonnet To Light

I write myself this nightly
Gesture of the turning
This should remind me to blink
And waken to your proximity
Which is continually present to the
Extent that nothing is not of you
Inhale a curve of dark foliage
Look to your shadow made by the moon
Drink a preposition
Which brings me nearer
To my present location
If words were put to that
Sentiment the sentence
Would read—

Protector #1 Against Ungainly Events

Against terror implicit in color alerts
Against agents of insured destruction
Fear breeding paycheck absence
Against psychological plague
Monitored media anti-pedestrian movement
Against hormones used for growth in normal children
Against golf and grass
Against demonizing golf and grass
Against public schools are forced to go corporate
Against dread of the news
Against placing responsibility—where?
Against forgetting your nature needn't be genocidal
Against monotony of daily endeavor
Against monotony in verse

Protector #2 Your Personal Amulet

This sonnet is your personal amulet
To be worn in instance of need
Or constantly held in the mind
Occurring here and elsewhere at this moment
This sonnet is sent without cunning
To cull a particular phrase from your lips
To enlist another protector
In this age of malcontent benefactors
Against an ironclad schooner
Feudal kingdom
Dismemberment by jubilant crowds
Strangely indifferent faces
Heat and dust besides
Suicide implicating others

Protector #3

Before the hermit people
When angels were robots
To operate happenings
A huge asteroid swam bravely through the water
His praying mantis–like jaw in the front
His sharp intertenacles broadly its engine turned on
They all turned on his boosters ·
Horn with a lasso on it in the tippy back
A "wavery" is a huge underwater cave where water bats live
On the rocky bottom sometimes water spiders
Suddenly a water landscape invaded
They were trapped
They had needed a very large breathe
Robotic-like forms formed in the water

From nothing is born nothing
This weeping day of possums
Crossing the night without
Pretense to homes
If you follow the boy with the curls
He will initiate you into his myth
Of the hermit people from which
We all evolved
If you follow his brother you
Walk in pre-mythic speech
Uttered with bodily syntax
Utterly trusting galloping
They follow the possum with no distance from beauty
Calling the landlord a game of broken garages

Protector #4

Against poetry from *The New Yorker*
Spiders on the potty
Menacing balloons
Nail broth
Against the time has come
When you all must go
And seek your fortunes
Against undone deeds
Against I wish that my pails
Could go of themselves
To the well and home again
Against whatever I strike shall
Break right off whatever
I pull shall become long

First kindergarten visit
Not to disrupt or
Learn anything either
Why we must apply
To public school
Lotteries in various
Divinations. Had a nice
talk with Jehovah Witnesses
So great a cloud
Of witnesses
But as for the dead
They are not conscious
Of nothing at all
Anything written on the forehead quivers

Josely Vianna Baptista Translation

Care enter verdant and cameras
Arias rigor and rill rapt
Vagram unwary mentors quiver
Desert recovers qualms
Treble risers and dogs leer
Serenade bell recant
Peeling rapid chores
Come O low rivet with outer
Spares and new sleep
Say luster cursive O second
Soul you wish to guest
With underbrush prate
Dolomite neon brio
No lit redundant loggia

40

Josely Vianna Baptista Translation

Poise cheque denounces desire nest
Deserts beaming immensity
Inexact chum knows nebula
Avenues, numens of Nevers
Eros coincides engendering
Equivocal semblance to five
Thumbs linger oblique sense
Same comic medium water
Blue which blights this day
Segue imp edifice needs
Moments and takes
Liquid menus
Incisive brief senders
Two lent vice tempo

Josely Vianna Baptista Translation

madrigal cold passage

traveling jasper

wrapped
in spades

mirage forms trill

vespers repent
present

aura mouth condenses
coat of pale sage

no soil stationed summer
lucid zenith

geometry beckons
iris dilates
microphone gale

Writing is a way to relate to recorded conversations
The albino rasta teen interrupts our intimate
$10-an-hour tea session—You're young
You steep too inhibited forgetting featureless parks
Sand parties and the neurosis definitely not
Bald-headed cross-legged silence or
You carry a tray up a few steps you take
Up the entire room with one hand gesture
You need to leave in order to assert your
Three-year-old tough-guy cape
The second night is for weeping (each morning)
As your disguise is untold
Hanging by his ankles is the only way to calm him
During this dim-minor spring fog

When you swallow it hurts my ears or
my consciousness suddenly shunted retracts
as if I had just been shoved into a closet
My practice is nowhere near—
yet I hold it up to light
The whole world is made
of bugs I say. I'm not a
person who used to report
pain has no substance and yet
using language as absinthe
she entered with a younger less
detailed version of herself
We are none of us immune
to gravity

Love Sonnet to Light

Is everyone a little in love with you
Or is it just me?
Did you write those flowering verses to a tree
Do I enter your stratosphere—
Can you speak with the dead
Parts of me mimicking you in a
Desperate attempt to remember
Is that glowering or glowing
Do I stand at the edge of the bed
Or sit as I mention your name
Becoming liquid, livid
Hidden, as if you were a person
I could embrace audibly
At any odd hour

Rilke Translation

Do anchor wren dice mandate mal
So insists veil, its ditch salt atman hoar
Under wending your twas branches
Under denim tasting eyes tank zoo reich
Nor eyes smaltz wander in wish
Church fall. Then its counting swine
Round dained older means mounds
Under sight of brittle eyes
Deign blizzards grist sow august
Under dear builder stern
Your dear wise numen
Webbing scented helmsman
Send a lone hamlet
Vines dirt agreement

Rilke Translation

When each nerve animal
So grave still wares
When thus zither under faire
Stemmed this burlesque lake
When garage maims sign matching
Microbe niche so Sir Hindrance
am watching
Dauntless Kant eyeing tousled falcon
Thanking bees audience randy ditch dunken
Under ditch be citizen
(nerve I'm lagging helm)
Umber ditch an alley
Leave zoo vervain
Wiles eyeing dank

Rilke Translation

Austere dear gesticulations embark
Sick redundancies, be legend warm and wheeze
And widen holster immense wilder seen
Dock for demi eastern toad came near fjord
Dame again risk dearth deigns rifle kraut
Under going I'm shorn
Under risqué dime stem fort
Die even erstwhile smelling
Ditch zoo sagging
Under ditch zoo tragic
Alleys grounds buckle
Under was seen seething strands
Cinder strike
Deigns to alter names

48

Two-Fourteenths Sonnet

This undressing at security checkpoints
Would never have gone over with the Victorians

Sonnet of Baron Marc Selys Longchamps

ASCIDIAN HEART

Manifests its presence by noises
knockings, a polite tangle of speech
Temperature below that of incandescent
Etruscan rooms lacking thought

A circular disc, usually wooden with metal rim
for discrete distance
A rumor or piece of gossip, often untrue
a sheet of white paper blotched and scrawled

Dearest secret, exquisitely wretched
flinty, impenetrable embryo blossoms
voice, a reed, white tipped
faults of love, one thousand to be well

One balm corrosive
vicissitude, tears of tea

Behind leaves he seeks
a ghost without cognition
Finds a scorpion in the woods
from which one still hears a car
A slug delivers
dogma and a mouse
skeleton is a millipede
Don't read those rejection letters
Too many classics
they might grow
spokes on you
Don't write letters to sonnets
or make dinner for abbreviations
from your hyperbolic dictionary

There's a fish eating a fish
That's the fish I want
Dinosaurs eating dinosaurs
Plants eat dinosaurs
I am three days old and very hungry
She clucks for us to run away
Daddy is very friendly
He lets me ride on his back
A pair of shoes went looking for someone's feet
Chugging upriver, a keel boat
Woodcocks on the leafy ground
Sisters have hatched too
Everywhere a dog might go
And the cracker was gone

Love Sonnet To Light

He who increaseth knowledge increaseth snow
Like the boy in the book not knowing
His own question, asks instead for directions
I wish to increaseth the depth of snows
With no language, step or plough
Without vocabulary for cold
Or the garment of your voice
Only buried I wish to ask
Where again beginning is possible
Shall I fear your presence opening a distance
I before did not compare to my desire
Or the light between your eyes
Which requires me
To look up from wintering

J's spoon
was golden
Because the light
shivered
An apple blushes
lemon
Lips water
hair pink
Her sleep is white
as rubies
(As snow dreams)
What does snow dream
about—
deeps in bed

Accretion

Cross talk bon mot articulator
Acquit careless hayseed haven't
Lowly gantry, compulsion by duplicate
Customhouse, cutaneous young swan
Prolong an omen or prone quotidian
A small nocturnal animal
A cluster of sonic answers
Dissolved in a given solution
Flung or flunk numbers
Collection of minute bubbles
Formed on the lightweight
Fingerholes or keys
Constitute nonchalant plush
Sluggard intent bolt

Bernadette Sonnet

Part subjunctive, the street is open
Someone sits behind you to record:
the trend spotter, the capitol of New Jersey
trench mouth or a plan having three
sides and a tribe
The sorting of patients, as in Triassic
To enter unlawfully long locks of hair
especially over each
trillium
related to a stream
of warp-knit fabric in trice
Two adjacent tones of a bird
A trick catamaran but having three
trolley cars of brass wind

Protector #5—Collage from California Recall
Ballot Statements

I am a recent immigrant like you
I dream like Martin
Luther King. I favor
the wonderful counselor
Buy a car
Since the days of the goldrush
Boy-friendly schools
Men's birth control
Greed has also caused
Adopted puppy or
kitten statements
Teach criminal penalties in school
Duplicate federal waste graduated
From California's abundant ocean power

Love Sonnet To Light

My love for you is not circumstantial
As an after-breakfast sonnet may
Summon the day but rather
Influential as the weather
I adorn myself with your greetings
Your circumstantial skin contains not
Your being but a form of your
Iconographic substance
With which you pierce all encounters
Anyone will permit
Themselves to be hidden within
You alliterate, you borrow time
From leaves, you calm me
With your voluminous absence

There is no line within time
Which will tell you for certain
Or certain telling only—o
To recognize your footing
There is no time within the line
I read in secret or write as a form
Of transport trespassing into
You of ribbony sight—please cut
Words only by hand or mouth
Syllables naysaying your search
For new leaves upon which to gather
The dotted guides to spring
Where you undress the sentence
In full light without apologetic green

Sonnet of Aristotle

ANCIENT SCARVES THROUGH THE
COUNTRY OF GREEN

Pluto is generally commissioned to sublime
idealists whose copper and a lookout destroy
a pond. He was prescribed, earthbound.
The thimble for which affectionate girlhood.

Fencers were obstinate and doghouses point
at inhumanity, interpolating their fields.
Violet starlets disseminate burgundy while
imagining the escapist gardens in the Academy

discussing phylogeny and hypothermia,
quarreling with the calligraphic disciples.
The froth of a chair is obscured by the
somnolence whose gull is grateful to end.

Scorpions in spite of their gravity
bridle a house, and seek crimson.

60

6/14 Donne Sonnet

I am a liturgy worsted made cupidity
Of elixir, and angelica spumone

I am a minute orb made subtly
Of rudiments, and innocent goblin

I am a little live oak made cupbearer
Of Elizabethan and angstrom sprawl

Sonnet Written with Lee Ann Brown

"Where does the vision take place?"—Nathaniel Dorsky

Are you going back to only
Drink deep of Miranda's hand
I love that sound identity
Momentum of milk
Close your eyes
Close your eyes again
Open your mammary memory
The way we examine our children
I feed in the night with a milkstick
A thief in the dark
Up against stained-glass windows
Were you dreaming in Germany backlit
It seems like a real picture
Vision taking place in the dark

In skirts and numbers
Morning glory plucked
Horses sleep in the castle
A striped stocking
Anchors a chair
The dragon has fallen
Onto his tongue
Curtains make sails
In broad swathes
Conduct light redly
Toward my eyes
Green leaf, brown seed
Russet stalk
And a knight lies under the miniature table

Somebody will pay a nice lonesome for you

A tick is great company

She was the oddest gazelle

The next time we go to those woods

Where we've never been before

We'll bring jars to catch scorpions

Some eat squirrel

When he sleeps he misses himself

The end of atomic bombs

As a choclatier knows it

Sorry, you're overqualified

Assuring a move toward

He doesn't resemble himself at all

A more synthetic musketeer

Love Sonnet to Light

For you
as real as person
unreal as reason
intentionally sightless

I run into the form of you
a sudden figure
in my gravity
dominion

A certain swiftness
in your presence
you lift the premises
from form of reason

A certain sightless scene, such is your sudden
presence—gravity entering sound

My rushing is so endless it seems
impossible to forestall
Even now, lettering my hand is obeying
a monitor of mind conflicting the
initial impulse to run
There is at all times so much
I often begin nowhere
or listly, as in to list
I cross off the unencumbered
Thereby ignoring the core
Blaming the limbs which could
not carry themselves
Circumference begs reference
unable to read without writing

Is there a storm inherent in your blemish parlor
Not to sleep with windows wide open
Certain books are not taken to bed
The room is encrypted silk
By way of ulterior your method sinks
Whose otherwise weather is brimming
Silence is a bright rest where focal
imaginings divide and prosper
Carry this neatly—
you of myself
If you offer
a phrase you repeat
without thought—two figures
immersed to the waist

If the noise doesn't stop when you turn on the light
You are of how many winters?
For readers of three and up
The mind sometimes a terrible souvenir
unlike his four-year-old face
in nest of night
whose test
of solitude
repeats the motion
Holding his hand to my face
I walk out of the bedroom
of again whose
forgotten impatience
Remembered the opposite of rushing

*Sonnet Beginning with a Line from
Norman Fischer*

All things transient
impermanent
He is running and
I'm holding his legs
He's lying
on his back laughing
Asking how long I will stay
They like pretending
They need saving
(mock falling in pillows)
Especially after my declaration
Always to aid
So they test the statement
Until I am tired

To walk at dusk
I miss my pedestrian life
I must gain foot with the children
Slowed by recent muggings
and demands of sippy cups
I fall into the car
So unsatisfactory
Today we hung B's skeleton
on our door, complete with
Each bone named
Jacob said, *you're precious*
I'm precious
You're crazy about me
At meditation I went and stood in the sukkah

I'm a poet with no preparation
Only invented moments
My husband is in France
Baby-sitter is ill
Husband returns to work
Children are ill
I've prepared this
without time
and yet like Charlie Buckets
I expect to enter
a place of no hunger
a realm of pure imagination
This makes me angry
Dear, poetic deficit

New York Sonnet

I'm on anyone's schedule
Out of ink and
inner perplexity rushes
This is my vacational headache
Too much small press and not enough
meals or sleeping. Constant
personages present, not those
I desire but rather those who
are affixed, affronted my tiny
time whose boxy sentiments
The countess of the letter is missing
in arbitrary attitude
Except for you
my invitation

New York Sonnet

If I miss anyone it's my fault
Having hidden messengers or time
or myself from
Those considerate longings
too easily disengaged
By unruly cohabitants of
this alphabetic landscape
When it is quiet I may exist
You collide in many rooms
where the cat does not stay
Forgive my reticence
which informs nothing of my interest
I am that animal where
Ushered quiet goes

New York Sonnet

Use that phrase as a seed
Your clotting premonition of me
Circling a destination
Travels backward in buses
or subways to Frank
who couldn't appreciate grass
unless your city framed my
city, a visit into your mattress
accompanied by a contagious curtain
a teacher who taught silence
Investigation of the 1,000 sordid images
which did not compose the view
Internally, your entrance, your text conspires
What is your mars, your venus, your moon (owned and earned)

F *Dictionary Sonnet*

Flung a blank leaf in the front or back
Collection of minute bubbles formed
on the surface of a short chain or curtain
Hanging from a pocket oxide to prevent further
flute players stock trading even or level with a
surface flush to rouse and cause to fly fluorescence
Squarely, to hurl or propel a fly casting or a bird
that feeds upon flux, a hand or set of cards
All of one folio, fobbing off the distance
between a focal point of a lens or mirror
and the corresponding principal flying
squirrel, generally believed to be
from outer space, a segmental arch which
carries the thrust of fly-by-night ruddy color

G *Dictionary Sonnet*

A very brief passing glassful
Twilight glob or globalism
Performed with a gliding effect
Such as sliding fingers rapidly
Over a tiny flash of light
Literary dusk or excessive gloat
A sphere on which is depicted
Ready and fluent glee
Gladsome or a small suitcase
Hinged to open into glacial
Epochs, glabrous given names
Such as gladiator having erect
Leaves and spikes of dress
Or manner

New York Sonnet

Offered a couch on 7th street
I tried to call you from the place
I first read your letters
I'm sitting with my history
Watching dusk as if it were
The same dusk (sane)
If you never leave your most significant
Settings how can you return to them?
Pull back and look at a face very near
The life of the subway is compressed
Persons create invisible space
When I lived here the mothers were somewhat invisible
Just as I have become elsewhere
Now they all jump out at me from the scenery

Philadelphia Sonnet

We're in the thick of early sentences
The hill is callow
On the outside
Awake in the gutter
We're in the thick of correspondences
Your gold dress glistens
On the outside of a circle you imagine
You are walking on the callow hill
Beside you are the thoughts which
Carry your features
Airports are airports
Callow is not gold
Except in certain light
You carry with you

Lee Ann Sonnet

Your sphere is contagion
For which I am grateful
As the Holland tunnel
trips me back to Newark
I recall your celebrity aura last night
Reading poems for Miranda in Philadelphia
Walking the poem carved into garden cement
We separate in body only
Your angelic smile is useful now
We're not alone then are we
In consultations with
Poetic constellations
Entrance of permissions
You are a field of mine

Sonnet of Baron Marc Selys Longchamps

ASCIDIAN HEART

Garbed in green
little thoughtless
faring through thicket
the ardent word
Single stroke is wrought
coiled around rookeries
in their rooms without shoes
troth plighters
brands and ashes
tournament
tussling
scribes
sash windows behind black
lilac, gold flowering

Double Sonnet of Princess Selys Longchamps

ASCIDIAN HEART

Blessed is she who arrives
said I, Orloff, to the talebearer
occupation: princess

Seated myself in stage coach under pretense of indisposition
I accompanied my husband to the town of _____
in the country of _____

A few incoherent words
A cordial
Thou wert fated

The carriage pulled up
(The Baron and our irreversible children)
They saw us through the plate glass window
absurdity of the peacock's tail
A voice which is not rectangular
the advantage of sex as sentient being

His blue trees surround me, she thought
being carried as an evolutionary remnant
Perhaps, what we lack as humans
this heart, upon white porcelain, is not to be believed

We are a flock of boxes fled our habitations
Whose hem length writes
Avow the fiction of my descriptive arrival
Tallow talebearer

Heart then is mesospheric
Rich or florid as ornamentation
any object of crescentlike outline
either of the two saclike
doublets, in the thorax

Absence Sonnet #1

for Brad

Those marks in the sky
Are signs of some ancient
Space explosion when
Only the sun and g-d were here
The page as lover does not interrupt
I thought I had some dread disease
It's called not sleeping
With you only illusory
When you come back
I'll learn to hand-letter the silence
You fly up
The spider said to the knight
Your skin of soft dough
In silky sight

Absence Sonnet #2

Certain cloth though very fine
Catches my hands and heels
As if my skin were rough wood
Tell me, tow-away tree work
If anyone misses these limbs
It is easy to be greedy in verse
Riches cost nothing here
And so are not prevalent
I'll place a garnet
Beneath your tongue for safe travel
Comfrey in your shoe
A rock is in my pocket
Take that pleading out of my shoe
Put it in the constancy bank, and go back to sleep

Sonnet of Baron Marc Selys Longchamps

ASCIDIAN HEART

Tiny only
oxymoron
flyest up till night
Compare that with an account
of the oyster
I had the wrong
revolver
the wrong man
Invertebrate belief
is a scattered aperture
The ascidian heart
Was thought not to exist
And so
He studied it

Absence Sonnet #3

Whose pen is this I'm writing with?
Jacob just had a woolly mammoth infant
Which he indicates by cradling his arms
Now he's dancing with girls at preschool
Romping with the crowd
Benjamin can't be bothered to notice
An impromptu drum session
He's too obsessively busy watching
An earwig under the hot dog shaped table
Later we leave ant poison for a friend
And take a walk among the eucalyptus
I've left his blue and green acorns in the car
Telling boys not to run with sticks is like
asking—who now will turn out the light for me?

14 Meditations Sonnet

Some snakes carry a sword

and a doctor's kit

Writing is a place to restively

repeat seasons

What an honor is a towel

or a fish's tale

A child's stone

persimmon shy

Plush salt

Folded intent

Radish translated

Dust parable

Haggling quaint narrow hills—are those my

children or pluck inhabitants?

Vinegar Sauce and Cauliflower (or 6/14 Sonnet)

efggf
efggefg
ggffg
fgfgf
socv
vcos

Silly or Funny Sonnet

Silly string and funny bone
What's the difference between
Silly and funny
Window sill and fun (house)
Funny knee
Funicular—up
Mountains on strings
Cables and
Silicasceous-made of silk
Cilliary
Singular fundable
Mandible edible
Tangible tangerine tantrum
Tenacious fabrication

Absence Sonnet #4

Time is an ingredient

Bulk seagulls

The difference between a Jakosaurous

And a Brontosaurus is that

A Brontosaurus doesn't have curls

I have a full-time life, really

The bad guys took over it

Can taking out the garbage be considered neglect?

What are you reading? Words words words

The heater sometimes dries my hair

In a theater with no heat you cross your legs

Hamlet was a woman, and you?

It's terrible my love to come home and find you not in bed

The moon is not believable—for its size—tonight

Gender & Wealth Sonnet (or Wharton's Buccaneers)

At Long Branch or Saratoga by the knowledge of
Intervening rheumatic earnings
America was elsewhere in strange railway pieties
Fomenter of your lovely frock
Author of only open fires
Insurrections of late thirties
Slipping her hand through the girl's thin flowers
Between delicately fluted wastefulness
There are no social traditions
Smoking enormous graces
To be introduced among the quick decisive more
Particular trifle brokers through the engagement
By novelty and by a slight flavor of thronging
From a distance with critical lighting her beribboned pillows

90

Sonnet while Listening to Kit Robinson Read

Does it matter who has written the line?
The line (I lay myself upon your planks)
Which I admire
Particularly as you read
But what would I think of a certain fondness for language
Without even an imaginary or dead person (attached)
Who has written/spoken
No one writes during readings in the Bay
Though getting wet is ulterior
I recognize that laugh at the back of the room
Or write a riff: *When unusual editions wake up in the morning*
They always say, good-day. Good-day, good-day, good-day, good-
  day (that is what they say) When an index-best-sellers-kings-
  consciousness-cats-chairs . . .
There is a surface you prepare
And a surface everyone sees

91

Science Sonnet for B.

A long cruel day of pipetting
Deep in hardened villagery
Reading "young men had dropped
their work and made for the safety of the hills."
He gave Vibart a meaning glance and went below
Moving small amounts of liquid
Not the embryos in the bottom
of the vials, tubes 40 x 40
I put it on a shaker
A love shack for bacteria
4,000 times for 24 tubes
I can't make any mistakes
If I spill a vial
I'll be a vile spiller

92

Sonnet Beginning with a Line from
Elizabeth Robinson

Teach a child to say
"Walks like a drunkard"
What do you do with a drunken
sailor early

in learning to walk

Or learning to come home

Newly to a leaf
There is no way to arrive alone
Where we all most wish to be

No going singly will go
far   but singing

you go in rows
invisibly linked
lines   walk with you

Sonnet for Elizabeth

O domestic atmospheric
Late-night pick-up of small plastic objects
Adorn yourself with language of dogs,
Spiders, prehistoric robots
Move with bodies attached to your own
In battle and cape
Command into their places
All relevant dates to walk not atop another
Break not fix not flooding
Unhinged sentences
Doors requiring your
Better-natured scribe
Welcoming your
True phosphorescent design

J Dictionary Sonnet

To squeeze tightly between bodies or surfaces
Whitish to dark green, a sharp projection on
A harsh metallic sound. Any of several shrubs
Or vines having fragrant opaque jaunts
A broad-mouthed oval-shaped jalopy
A person who cleans and maintains January
Vigilant in guarding trousers made of
mock, scoff, or sneer. Using auxiliary
receptacles for holding vocabulary peculiar
to crushed or boiled javelins.
The junction between juvenile delinquents and
To cross a street in a heedless manner
As from concussion, an archaic jest
Which feeds upon the foliage of journalism

Pre-Election Lunar Eclipse

Darkening acclaim of oblong
Ecru, pertaining to edelweiss
The past participle of most rapturous
Radar or sonar, economical
Currents at variants with the light
Of the European common market
The branch of biology dealing with
A cream puff filled with white
Wooly leaves, a small whirlpool
Having excessive eclogues
The supposed emanation from the body
Ebullient vulcanite
Eavesdropping from various tropical trees of Southern India and
   Ceylon
To surpass or outshine

A voice through time is discourteous to age
Or age is not what it appears
Or passing a window makes use of my hand
Or all persons or throats must we double
the space of the evening
by listening as we write?
The room where the sounds emerged
was hidden behind othering
So the personal adds pleasure to years
elapsed in no other spine
I'm listening beneath the word
to where the poet is someone
Will this befall all?
You seem somewhat not alive

97

Triple Sound Sonnet

I

Gathering flowers
in the field of Enna
Avuncular interest
Like an uncle
all day crunched
over the loose shingle
Why once I was hiding
in a loft
In a faintly antiquated elegance
White tulle of course
Nothing will ever replace waters
of Babylon
A heavily
whale-boned dress

II

Gathering hours
in the shield of inevitable

Rectangular seamstress
Trike a funnel
All may lunch
over the goose thimble
My ounce eye buzz chiding
in soft
Greatly anticipated eloquence
Blight jewel remorse
Winning ill ever efface
Daughters of
Avalon
A heave ale honed tress

III

Father our in
field of enviable
Rectitude seething
Stricken fumble
Doll made jump
Heave whose windmill

Mine outer oracle was
Childling in rafts
Grape anti pasted elevators
Height cruel remove
Hitting will
never pronounce
Heathers (of)
Avail

I hold your book in my hands and imagine you reading
Using words distinctly as truth not often enough expressed
Jubilant to do so careful not to confuse longing with admiration
Since attention is penetration or a page or word longer lasting
Unless we were both someone else in a less
complicated ethical humor or species
Thus, praise is a form as erotic as a smile secreted sent
My 2-year-old playing guitar for his 5-year-old flame
He broke into her universe by standing close and staring
Age is only anything—comparisons make nothing of youth
Losing hair may be adoring
What this means is
if you have a body
only love is possible

One-Minute Sonnet (minus coupling)

Take me home with you as a book
goes to bed beside me
The mind knows fluently little of love
If I keep a given notion
I go to sleep
If you argue into wakefulness
we wrestle
And that is how to learn the name
of your other self
You might have written this
I certainly did not
but don't let that stop you

100

Sonnet Without Looking

I love you because
it's easier than resisting
as I trip over your shoes
You write adoring letters
Read to me in bed
Wake me unexpectedly
Though you aren't awake are you?
In another country
I should be sleeping
there—on a rice mat with you
but the children need beds
Anything can be turned
even from this distance
my eye toward your face

101

Chance Meeting Couplets

I've been having babies
And you?

The way a photograph
shows you nothing

Where are you
my minute?

Magenta morning
pierced with bare branches

As they sleep
they move intelligently

Take this kiss
I could thank you in another way

Our secret worlds are crucial
to all our public meetings

102

P Dictionary Sonnet

He (or she) painted (it) formerly
Any evergreen, conebearing pistolwhip
A game played by two, three, or four
Pirates conveying baseless fancy
Used for trimming edges and seams
Of light sailing vessels
One of those who first enter or settle a
Long series of pipes, having leaflets
Arranged on each side of a common
Piscatorial whirling about on one
Pious foot or an archaic ant used
In singing for a teammate in the brain
Of all vertebrates which revolves when
Blown upon a pin

103

Why Wolves Aren't Famous

It's not an idea (I forgot)
What should the title be?
I'm tired of pure form
Pass me that framework
The knight of the ox is very famous
He destroyed the dragon's cape
All I know about capes is water
Ghost and mud bring it back to life
Now eat your pancakes and stop
dreaming about syrup crystals
The flowers have pink, yellow, purple all I know
You might find a password
in one of them so look carefully
Did you write this in a whispery tone?

How About Some Chair for Breakfast

Please come back I love you more than any horse
Don't poke yourself
Have some prehistoric fun
That will show me where to bite
Is he really married to a poem?
Is yesterday a pharmaceutical?
Are you having a mental affair
with your favorite pack of lies
Just to avoid the holidays as if
that made it clear which ones I was referring to?
For instance are you commanded to be so intoxicated
you cannot tell a woman from a man?
You will be chastised in the afterlife
for every pleasure which you do not partake now

105

Sonnet Beginning with a Line from Jordan Davis

I'd like to be a calligraphic homestead for vertigo
Where the sheep dance in pairs
and the shepherd is really your soft palate
Talk to me of synapses and remolding the brain
We can learn and crib from the father of all robots
I'm a knight with a big red baby in my arms
too many years old
Preschool conference concerns: social? kindergarten?
Why all persons die. Except mommies and daddies
Sobbing at bedtime having taken too much
Wonkavite and becoming a minus
Is that why we must sleep horizontally
To cancel ourselves out
In scarlet town with you

Sonnet at the End of the Yellow Pigalle Notebook

I should marry you, I thought upon our first
meeting before which my sister had poured
espresso down my throat and dragged me to
the club med disco. There you were, jumping
up and down like a star. No one but we
believe we did yoga on the beach until 2 a.m.
You lost the key to your room and I pretended
to be sad until you found it
You said goodnight to dream a wish
fulfillment letter I'd written.
It wasn't you smoking, unshaven
my family insisted, walking in a suspiciously
tan and tight way. On first parting you suggest
we try a psychic writing exercise at precisely o'clock

One-Half Sonnet

Do sheep have laps?

Is Moomin a cow?

Do hippos swing on ropes?

Corral covered with grasshoppers

touching their bottoms

One hyena cocktail with mites

tail bitten off

108

So as not to wake you I undress on the stairs
Bulb extinguished as I write like a bee
upon this controversial table
My absence is something
I cannot explain by white space
and yet your look misunderstands
what the children resemble as they sleep
Remembering the charm of responsibility
is as inexplicable as human form
Further than habits gathered or dropped
There is no permanence in
devotion of that kind which does
not require a guardian even in rest
You may undo or walk away from anything else

109

Thoughts on an Essay

If you again allow yourself to palliate
I will do something even he would be content with
Leaving behind divine right of kings
What induced those people to burn houses
He had such and such mistresses and governed badly
There were certain men writing books at this period
He killed many people because he was a very great genius
These conversations made people happy or unhappy
It could be quite a mistake to suppose that this is mockery
If another force is put in the place of divine power
The peasants' contention is irrefutable
Then it should be explained what that force consists of
How carefully I raise my arm
To recognize a dependence not perceived by your senses

Rilke / Duino Elegy Translation

Where when itch shriek hoards
mica den us dear angel
Or nudging gazelles siblings are named
Eye might puzzle and hers
each version won signing
Starkest desire. Den of shining
first nights always
these shrinking lichen
afghan den wire notch grade estrogen
Under weird bewildered snow veiled
as glassy Versailles
Zoo snoring, eye jaded angel is kreplach
Under so very itch mitts den and
very shucks den lock rough

111

*Rilke / Duino Elegy Translation Written
with Brad Davidson*

Where when is several
My garden is mulched
full of angel
Or maybe not
I'm selling gefilte fish
do you want some?
I grew it in my plot full of embryos
I'm just joking
I went to the Anfang theater with Grady
I'm bewildered
The gelato there is not
so good in the store
At Angel's house it's really good
I want to lick it

112

Love Sonnet to Light (3/14)

Your secret self I already
have seen lurking and more comely
rows and rows of words become you

After-Shower Sonnet

Before dressing don't
cheat on me in my dreams
especially from a distance
Below I hear four boys
breaking mountains into breeze
Before we go to the happiest place
on earth I must remember my
own special paradox
While dressings are everything here
Undressing is everything any other place
we go so let's go there
not fruitfully, but secretly
and hide from the plastic pots
and smoke of their diagramming snores

114

After-Sonnet Shower

Regularity breeds intimacy
Who says it has to be good
Not us but this hidden impulse
Mind's reckless freedom
To count, to undo buttons, to perspire
Clean backward full-length
Permanent imprint
Vertical welt
There was no body and yet
exclusively
her memories continued
Intimacy breeds time
Who says not us
To count backward

115

War and Peace Sonnet

Well there "ing" him
To see what egoists lovely
Police ran with mirth
In a whisper, shabby shapeless shoes
And vacancies occur inappropriately
Eagerly anticipating his medicine
Leaning against a column months before
I am finishing my second rather useless
Moments of carefully fastened tape
What your excellency means wallows
A high blue Vienna coach with several
Half an hour, only slightly wounded
The general frowned as though destroying behind him
The other side of the river in tunics

116

Variation 116

Let me not to the marrow of truant minds
Admit the impenetrable. Lozenge is no lounge
Which alternates when it altercation finds
Or bends with the renaissance to remount
It is a fixed marketplace
That looks on Temperate Zones and is never shaggy
It is the starlet to every wandering barmaid
Whose worship's unknown, although her hype be taken
Lown's not timocracy's foist, though rosy lisps and Chekhov
Within its bending sibyl's compote come
Loxodromic alters not within brief hound's tooth and weevils
But bears it out even to the eft of dowagers
If this be erythema and upon me provincial
I have never writhed nor no maniac was ever louse

117

Why I'm Not a Paintbrush (or L. A. Sonnet)

Why in attitude you stood in a doorway
Not willing to concede not willing to
do anything but spar or stab your
index finger with a sewing needle
in order to extract something there all along
The way monographed gifts epitomize a
place I'd rather not be
The way entering a certain leaden house
The way a child mistakes car for driver
He stands clutching a plastic steak to his chest
Fencing with a chopstick
Asking, what does oblivious mean?
and you wonder why I refuse to be transfixed
By your gratuitous dramas

118

Eleven-Fourteenths Sonnet

You have bad camera karma
Jacob the trouble book
The leaf looks like an ancient fossil
How young is younger than one?
Don't take one from the bag
I'll give you a
train you can eat
Four more for the door
I want to be a race car
or a race car driver
I will not fly over the water

Scarlet puppies run
It looks like it's time to read books
Brine rhymes with Kai
The cup doesn't go on your head
Two boys with mouths full of eggs
What do we do with toes on the table?
Jacob looks like a unicorn
With a blue-cup horn
Your fork is not a weapon
Nana lives up in a plane
Because it's foggy in Benjamin's brain
Are you a newt today?
A dinosaur eating a weathervane
Doggies eating houses

120

If you are drinking milk
then you are a fisherman
because fish don't drink milk
Fish drink water
instead of other drinks
They live in streams
and streams don't
have other drinks
It is not real
It cannot flap its wings
I'm done being alone in another country
I'm in L.A. being blown off by my grandmother
Would you like some light?
This is my invisible name

Jacob's Guesses

Lime butter
House butter
A peanut-butter
car
Can I eat it?
Something round
A beer
A bear
The light
He needs to close his
Eyes and smell it
He can't guess
I have to tell him
In the butterfly bag

Glad you could make it web head
Tent 3 is full of bats and snakes
with Electro and the Sandman out of commission
Zeus turned the seven sisters into birds
Thrown over cliffs or burned a little
in old windmills
The sickle lion head is formed by six stars
And they lifted their scaly little cheeks
Jayko faces the evil Vladek in the grand tournament
Match each symbol to the correct letter
Sheepshanks, Laceleg, Balthazar
The Mallards called on Michael every day
Michael fed them peanuts
Come closer you pesky wall-crawler

123

In Chinese astrology you are a snake
but at home you are a kitty-knight
You don't have any bunny in your body
You ate a bunny but you're not a bunny-king
To make a person you need two people
Otherwise you'll just get a big belly
And the baby will never hatch
Your favorite food is syrup
Jewel Jim "the pig," our pet caterpillar,
Red, gray, yellow, and black
Is searching for a bramble leaf to eat
My rice bowl is not full
Jacob kicked me in the top of my nose
We pushed each other off of the couch

124

Sonnet of Aristotle

GALILEO WROTE OF THE GRAND DUCHESS

Of spiders that are smooth and weave
a close birth
She allots to form teeth and tusks.
I mistake every plausible

experience of the senses.
The sun itself is expressed by dots,
essentially a collection
of longer-legged photographs.

Individuals form a chain and each clings
to the shell of the one beneath
as practically all theories
confined to wilderness areas.

Whether the earth rotated or was at rest
or else

125

I'm so embarrassed when I remember how I insisted
How many can I admire to help?
Is there a number which may finish desiring action
or is attraction a simple form of waking?
How many eyes at a time do you slumber
Perplexed by seeing respondents
and why you won't believe what you've written
For instance a stream of steady birds in rain
involve changing your shirt
in a cold room
Only blue in shivers
Why you won't repeat
fragile nests
and so listen

126

The air makes you cruel
Birds fly backward through the train
Thus to record in sentences impressions from beds
upon which lay what I recognize in your mouth
A window absconded trapped between a cat
on the other side of the glass, and the wreath which
frames the same candles on your winter table
Stained wood spoke to the flat lying clouds
His eyes stood nearer to causation
of person and pleasantly pressed a few paces apart
No distance then could interrupt
such coughing of reason
Your wayside plate of music
unencumbered by sight

Glottal Sonnet

I grew up getting in a car

He's clearly what they didn't

He goes the way three times as long

While I wait

A face looking out from a photograph isn't

One in each hand, walking

These are my last

And canceled singing

Crowding a "holded" flower arrangement

Stranger's breath on wrist

A shadow sits next to me

Her book my uncle

Small towns being

Festive water

I'm a bunny
in a human suit
so people
don't try to eat me
when I go shopping
Is it not winter
at his house?
Daytime never ends
What is that living
in our curtain
gray and yellow and red
Our neighbor rakes a tree
Does an apple cry
done going down?

One of the Many Advantages of Furnaces

When I am a big man
I will play with the plunger
I'm being bitten in bed
The title is never indicative
Is being a toddler like
Perpetual morning sickness
Jelly blobs as big as Chanticleer the rooster
Nutritionally speaking
Are you being respectful
Of your child or simply stupid
Knock knock, go away fox
Don't cry it's just a joke
You called at absolutely the worst moment
I'm busy playing predatory games

1968 Flu Strain (Four Missing Lines Infected)

This is a telescope
Made out of a turkey
Sound of your hair
Falling onto the couch
It is intimate to carry
your book around
and the ten best
made-up animals follow
You are an "el-e-ant"
Because you are gray

131

(Divergent Couplets)

Can you pickle anything?
How about a building?

Seen any praying mantises on leashes in the garden
Where we walk and watch for maelstroms?

132

One Plus Couplet Sonnet

I search every book for the dedication
I must make as myself
Edge of a page finds me and is naught
If I sleep on the outskirts of a near gathering
I have come to enter my own future
heart where the old friend who
fears is dismissed to stand nearer
Where we are all gathered to pick up our children
therefore we must have access to
patience thrust
either easily or with much difficulty
I walk into another landscape to
discover the person possessing the
key to my rest utterly sobbing

133

One-Half Sonnet

Gobble is a kind of goblin
Jacob's love is Jacob's
At the playground
My eyes turn white
You don't love every lamb you see
They are almost hollow
Birds enjoy the air

134

Catalhoyuk's Place in History
(Two-Fourteenths Sonnet)

O late sanctum of gold-eyed snake

Pink construction paper upon which you eye me

Sonnet Beginning with a Line from Ted Berrigan

The wind's wish is the tree's demand
Demands of three and five or
Two children and a mirror
The child's wish is a raccoon kiss at the door
Black asphalt parting while standing in line
The mirror's wish, demands of three and five
Or to mind less the wind, to walk with
Not to counter or to separate wind from air
Child from number, counting from substance
Demand the wind or the number to walk
Not hurried but an invigorating scruple or
Who to be on the back of a book read at bedtime
Or breakfast, to sing before, as they sit
Little curls without numbers, at a table

Valentine Sonnet

With your permission day is red

Less blindly as we turn waking

Welcoming what awaits consciousness

Newly as day requires

Again our bodies pulled apart and into

Motion containing objects, form

supplying destinations of thoughts and

macro-pull of diminutive sphere

We arrive again upon a walk

Chasing four small legs upon a medicinal

bridge. We read the names, verdant composers

Winter garden, steps count the light

where witch hazel guards our coming

Lengthening of concentration

Prostitution + Black Holes

A city combs madam's black fleeting thing
For names escort a service including everyone
Trove set out for men entering Mercury
Lovelorn and lenient penalty elite
That a star is doomed if it ventures too close
Operating a house of assignation
Thrown off course by encounter
Stellar tidal disruption
In the elegant second-floor foyer of
Gravitational influence in the wrong
Neighborhood ledger, mainly forever
Surveillance tapes and 8,500 pages of
Chagrined clientele
That doom is a star, if it ventures, swallows

Boy is body sans d
Her hair straightens
Normalcy maidens
A yellow wrapper
Becomes cross-stitched
Lip-age equipment for
Categorizing filmic lids
Come home electric suspect
Makers of admission
Backward in an underheated
Person torpid stations
Ventricle balm utterance
Inscribe is scribe not inward
Compel—cell comp plenty

Sonnet + 2

Despite irrevocable household differences
Despite your timely innocuous cutting paper birds
Variable remedies to silt peppering
Narrowness of apothecaries
His inability to stand or sit in front of a painting
He must run toward a canvas of red
The desire to touch what he perceives as
Dragon fire, seeing figures everywhere in battle
Was it something you touched at the zoo
Or fossil hunting debris symmetrically pressed
Against your once translucent cheek
Please prescribe for me a remedy to the intolerable
I miss my extra immunities brought on by
Childbearing, now humbly expired
Is this the afternoon for hyena viewing
Or just another dinner of peas?

140

Love Sonnet to Light

I want to remember my nature
As you know it
All unthought
everywhere to go
Forget singularity
The nice thing about concentration
is that no one can look
in on how you are doing
I covet the invisibility of the act
or cessation of action—depending
Perhaps my only true privacy
unless you consider sleep
nestled against another like-minded
invisibility as an action

No hopping on your head
No jumping on your tongue
No screaming blue
No pushing yourself over
No scratching the letter "E"
No biting beetles
No dropping hiccups
No grappling houses
Never hit never fall down never hit yourself
Never put water on the ground
Never knock yourself down
No running inside a grape
Chew up my dark day
Q has a little tail

Fossil Man (a dinner sonnet)

The diamond missile
Is sticky—staying for dinner
He likes everything raw
You are scared snail—the diamond entry
Out of the city and well provided for
We brought Manuel Noriega a snowglobe
She wrote a president a letter
The diamond ship wrote a letter
Lava pal—I'd help you
I want to write to the fossil hunter
Can I have a fossil man?
I'll color red paint on him
A fossil man that is just bones or
One who digs fossils

Daddy, say a sonnet
The lamb stands up
Benjamin sit down
The lamb stands all the way up
Worked into an iron arch at his entryway
Very cool, but then you fall off
Two days later with no alternative
the lamb, making its way
through the senate
This is all about the lamb
An unadorned "c" refers to alphabet A
whereas the curlicue "c" represented alphabet B
Quote, the Aryan brotherhood "ba ba ba ba ba"
Confer message from Chris to move on DC

144

The queen ant flew off of our roof
Flowers are purchasing color
I send you a kit for impulse
A cloud forest fastened with crofts
The bat plant and an orchid
Tendered yellow
For you I have refurbished
The conservatory of flowers
We sit beside the pitcher plants
balmily carnivorous
For me you have begun building
upon the site of Adolph Sutro's former home
Overlooking the ocean
above Seal Rock

145

We are somewhere abroad in formal attire
You eat raw meat from your hand in the street
On the way to an elaborate dinner where you
Know everyone and an intricate system of
Communication using small round silver
Hand mirrors with which to speak indirectly
And read the expressions of others covertly
Like the Victorian language of fans
Everything you express regarding yourself
Is untrue. I have no mirror, nor do I know
How to engage in this type of silent talk
You hold yours discretely close to your body
Angling at the level of the table
Laughing, unconcerned

That rose got bigger in the night
because inside there is no sun
There's a paper axe in his crib
Now you will only make pictures of leaves
What was the bug's name?
He shoots prisms onto the porch
A rose as big as a chandelier
He asks for his sword
when he wakes
You will only make a shadow in the shade
another daddy longlegs
I want to get everything down from that dresser
that we've never had before
That's because I'm a poem-faced boy

147

Sonnet (one quatrain)

Your hands are dirt
Your head is dirt
Your tummy is dirt
I did put my own head back on

Love Sonnet to Light

The only one I undescribe
Like every tale which
in its telling is told
I walk about your entrances mentally
not fitting or fastening
No cloistering
no gathering oneself to meet you
There is only you unseen
And I in my imagined
stammering chamber
As if you had not inhabited
the space of my worry
As if not even this circling thought
became your ornament

Love Sonnet to Light

Equanimity isn't my pond
I'm not unfluttered, nor non-corporeal
I do questionable things
when pulled
I seek the opposite
of dispassion
Abiding attachment
An intimate and personal
attempt to ignite
This isn't my idea, it's borrowed
from a body treading upon the earth
in seasonal patterns
before this body
and before the many—before

150

Nine-Fourteenths Sonnet

(Forgive me
This is the only
place I may
speak to you
freely
As conversation
is not what I
intend
in talk)

151

Brood X

Cicada drinks via radio
Seventeen years underground as nymph
a circadian sentence
feeding on sap from tree roots
scratching its tymbals, dug out
to sing, molt, mate
Just think of a giant loyalist poker face
Marking itself for birds
cinquefoil, not loose-leaf
beseeched to change metallurgy
Wakened from larval slum
Prime number cycle
most numerous
because they seek no completion

The Permeable "I," A Practice

How elastic is form?

This is a collaborative experiment in time. Consider ways to rearrange your time and space tendencies as a method (write yourself out of whatever existing parameters you fall into) and see what happens.

As a parent of two small children I invent time in order to work. Thus the one-minute sonnet. Thus the collaboration with the kids. And finally after many years of controlled circumstances, the allowing in of all voices, all time. Deep and scattered fragments of time. Loud and physical time. Someone else literally pulling you out of your chair. Writing in your sleep, or falling face first (exhaustion) into the keyboard while writing, as Maureen Owen so wonderfully describes in her essay in *The Grand Permission*.

I have collaborated with the daily news, with other poets, with the bumpiness of days passing in real time and with children's voices, books, and sense of time. I have drawn from devotional practices the sense of the poem as an offering—it is beyond ownership—what may be given now. When time is unhinged anyone or thing can speak: the dead, the imagined, the dictionary, the found.

There is an openness I attempt to enter as an experiment, as a salute to, or recognition of time passing.

This is a wake up and discover another year disappearing tactic. It's a surrender. Upheaval. It's the tower card in tarot which means the ground beneath you literally shifts (and not slightly). It's the painful slap on the back with a wooden block while you are doing the dishes. It's the question whispered, "*Mommy are you meditating?*" and the little body, little voice climbs onto your lap as you sit and your old vision no longer exists. And your new role is more invisible for its commonness and more challenging and exquisite for its namesake than ever seemed possible.

This is not a lament, but rather a plea against the invisibility of the guardian.

A plea against invisibility or blindness to whatever circumstances you find yourself within. The circumstance may also become, inform, or suggest the poem and the practice.

All mental states, traps, games, and assemblages are welcome here. My sonnets are an approachable unruly gathering. What the poems have in common is that they practice permeability.

I think of the modern sonnet as an increment of time within a frame. Something that often physically fits into a little rectangle (but not in thought). Something you can utter in one long convulsive breath or hold in your palm. When my hand covers the page, it disappears. It's a controlled measure of sound and space within which one can do anything.

This book is an invitation.

Notes

4. All dictionary sonnets are based on the same chance procedure, which I call a dictionary divination. Open the dictionary at random. Write a poem using only the text that appears on the facing pages in front of you.

17. Altered version of first two lines are taken from the poem "A semi-permissive environment" in the book *Zero Star Hotel* by Anselm Berrigan.

19. "Post-Election D Sonnet" was written in reference to the U.S presidential election of 2004.

26. The Baron Marc Aurule Gracchus Selys Longchamps, was the last scientist, before my husband, Brad Davidson, to study the evolution of the ascidian heart. He was born in Paris in 1875, and died in Brussels on May 11, 1963. The cover images on this book (which look to me like both commas and diaristic embryos) are based on photographs from my husband's developing ascidian larvae.

33. The "protector" sonnets were conceived to be worn as amulets—guarding one from all manner of current cultural maladies.

39. Homophonic translations from Josely Vianna Baptista are from the book *On the Shining Screen of the Eyelids*. Text is in Portugese and English. Translations are by Chris Daniels.

45. Homophonic translation inspired by poems from Rilke's *Book of Hours*.

55. This poem was written for Bernadette Mayer after a reading she gave in San Francisco in 2004. We were having dinner at

an Italian restaurant and considering the mysterious occupation of "trend spotter." Thus, this unlikely list of trends.

56. This piece was composed entirely from the California recall ballot in 2005, filled with absurd statements from masses of hopeful governors.

59. Aristotle wrote this sonnet using the translation technique of mis-seeing his own text. He took off his glasses and had a friend hold his manuscript just beyond arms length. He could almost see individual letters but could not exactly read them. He then dictated the new text to a third friend who acted as his scribe.

60. This fractional sonnet was composed employing various chance operations on the opening lines of John Donne's "Holy Sonnet Number 5." Donne's lines are:

I am a little world made cunningly
Of elements and an angelic sprite

61. The quotation from Nathaniel Dorsky is from his book *Devotional Cinema.*

62. This is an "I see" sonnet written with children. Only things you can literally see are allowed into the poem.

68. Italicized lines taken from Norman Fischer's book *Success,* from the poem "Sunday 4 March."

69. A *sukkah* is a temporary dwelling constructed during the Jewish festival of *sukkot.* It is made of branches and decorated with fruits and leaves.

70. Charlie Buckets is a character from Roald Dahl's book *Charlie and the Chocolate Factory.* Also taken from this book is the phrase "a world of pure imagination."

73. In reference to "Frank"—see Frank O'Hara's "Meditations in an Emergency," in *The Selected Poems of Frank O'Hara.* The "thousand sordid images" is from Elliot's "Preludes."

78. This poem was written after a reading at the Kelly Writers House at the University of Pennsylvania, by me, Lee Ann Brown, and India Radfar in October, 2003. The poem carved into the garden steps is "The Quality of Heaven" by William Carlos Williams.

80. Olga Orloff, a Belgian princess, met the Baron Marc Selys Longchamps in Naples. They were married in 1905.

89. This poem is collaged entirely from Wharton's text.

90. This poem was written while listening to Kit Robinson read at Moe's bookstore in Berkeley, 2004.

92. First two lines taken from the poem "Experiments with Gravity," from the book *Pure Descent*, by Elizabeth Robinson.

95. There was a lunar eclipse October 27–28, 2004, the last eclipse before the U.S. presidential election of November, 2004.

104. "Please come back, I love you more than any horse" is from the children's book, *Little Black*, by Walter Farley. To become so intoxicated that one cannot distinguish man from woman (or good from evil) is a Jewish custom during the festival of Purim. The last two lines are derived from Talmud.

105. The first line is taken from the ongoing project *Million Poems Journal* by Jordan Davis. "Wonkavite" is a substance that makes you younger in *Charlie and the Great Glass Elevator*, by Roald Dahl.

107. "Moomin" is a character in many of the delightful children's books by Tove Jansson, who was born in Finland on August 9, 1914, and died on June 27th, 2001.

109. This sonnet is collaged from an introductory essay on Tolstoy's *War and Peace*.

113. The "shower" sonnets are inspired by Bernadette Mayer's experiments. Here is an attempt to invent time: write a sonnet while standing wrapped in a towel.

115. This sonnet is collaged from Tolstoy's *War and Peace*.

116. This piece is based on Shakespeare's sonnet 116. N + 7 and various other chance operations are employed. Nouns are replaced with those that fall seven entries down in the dictionary.

117. The title of this poem is inspired by Frank O'Hara's poem "Why I'm Not a Painter."

135. First line is from Ted Berrigan's poem "XVII" from *The Sonnets*.

144. This poem was written for Brad Davidson at the sites mentioned, all in San Francisco, including the Conservatory of Flowers in Golden Gate Park. Opened in 1879, it is the last remaining wood-frame Victorian conservatory in the country. It was refurbished in 2003.

151. May of 2004 marked the dramatic and prolific emergence of three cicada species dubbed Brood X after a 17-year cycle underground.

In *The Permeable I, A Practice*: the essay mentioned by Maureen Owen is titled, "When as a Girl on the Plains of Minnesota," from *The Grand Permission*, an outstanding collection of essays by women poet-mothers.

About the Author

Laynie Browne is the author of five previous volumes of poetry, most recently *Drawing of a Swan Before Memory*, which won the Contemporary Poetry Series from the University of Georgia Press in 2005. She is the recipient of the 2007 National Poetry Series award, chosen by Alice Notley. With others, she curated poetry reading series at The Ear Inn in New York City from 1992–1995 and as a member of the Subtext Collective in Seattle from 1996–2001. She has taught poetry in the schools as a visiting artist in New York City and Seattle, and has taught creative writing at the University of Washington, Bothell, and Mills College. She currently lives in Oakland, California.